MOSCOW
MITCH

A TRAGIC POLITICAL SATIRE IN
THE MANNER OF MODERNIST
EXPERIMENTAL LITERATURE

By Citizen XX

MOSCOW MITCH
Copyright © 2019, Citizen XX. All rights reserved.

N.B., This humorously profane broadside satirizes and parodies
real-time political events. Real time information changes
rapidly. At the time of publication, the commentary in this book
was based on commonly-found news items, the veracity and
interpretation of which will invariably change as events evolve.

Cover and Book Design: Nauset Press.
ISBN: 978-0-9907154-7-4

Apologies to Gertrude Stein,

specifically her *Sacred Emily* poem,

and barnyard animals, too.

Tip of the hat to George Orwell's *Animal Farm*.

MOSCOW MITCH

- Brendan Dunn
(Mitch's former top aide,
Akin Gump, LLP)

- Hunter Bates
(Mitch's former chief-of-staff,
Partner Akin Gump, LLP)

- Steve Mnuchin
(US Treasury Department Head)

- Elaine Lan Chao!
(Mitch's "Roommate"*,
US Transportation Secretary)

- Jim Breyer
(Mitch's brother-in-law,
venture capitalist)

RUSAL
(world's second largest aluminum company)

- Oleg Deripaska
(Oligarch, President, Rusal)

- Len Blavatnik
(Oligarch,
22.5% ownership in Rusal)

VLADIMIR PUTIN
(Russian President)

- Yuri Milner
(venture capitalist)

- Trumpo
(Putin's little buddy,
Mitch's big buddy,
US president)

*Moscow Mitch has "humorously" described his wife as his roommate.

Moscow Mitch is a Moscow Mitch is a Moscow Mitch. *Moo.* Moo cow. Mitch milks his Moscow moo cow. Mitch milks his Moscow cashcow. Milk. Mitch. Milk. Mitch milking his moo cow from Moscow to make cash. Making a cashcow. Cash. Milk. Milk = Cash. Moscow Mitch. *"Moo, moo,"* says the cashcow. Moscow Mitch is a Moscow Mitch is a Moscow bitch to the mooing of millions of milk cows. Millions of cashcows. How many?

It's an estimated 22.5 million or so. Wow. That is a lot of teats. A lot of cashcow teats to milk. *Moo.* How many fingers does Moscow Mitch have? How many fingers are needed to milk a moo cow, a cashcow? Many fingers, it would seem. How many fingers do human beings usually have? Usually 10. 10 fingers. 5

fingers on 2 hands. How many fingers are needed to milk one cashcow? For most humans, about 10 fingers. Wow, how does Moscow Mitch do it? Does he have more than 10 fingers? Maybe he uses some Russian fingers to help milk all of those cashcows. *Moo, moo.* Hear the cows crying, hear knuckles cracking on the cashcow teats. **Gold** coins clunking into the milk pail. *Clunk.* **Gold**. *Clunk.* **Gold**. *Crack. Crack. Clunk.* Don't overfill the milk pail or it will spill!

Moscow Mitch is a Moscow Mitch. What does that even mean? It means he doesn't mind if the pail overflows. It means more cash from a cashcow for him. He will make a bigger pail. Fix it, Mitch! Fix that pail! Make it bigger! The bigger it is, the more it can be filled. *Moo, moo.* More milk, more cash. More cashcows make more clunking coins. Moscow. More moo cows make more milk. Both go in a pail. How much milk can a human being drink in a day? Maybe 8 glasses. How much milk can Mitch McConnell drink? Moscow Mitch has an infinite thirst. He is one of the thirstiest men around. *"Slurp, slurp,"* goes Moscow Mitch. "I could drink from this Russian cashcow all day!" and he does. Moscow Mitch drinks from his cashcows. His thirst never abates. *Slurp, slurp.* Mitch is sipping from his cashcows. Moo. *Clunk.* **Gold**. *Crack, crack. Clunk.* Moo. **Gold**. *Crack. Crack. Slurp, slurp. Clunk. Clunk. Clunk.* **Gold**.

"It's all mine," Moscow Mitch thinks. "I can never have enough. I don't want to share any of my milk." Moscow Mitch, Moscow Mitch. All the cashcows. All the moo cows. One is not enough. 1 million is not enough. 10 million is not enough. 100 million is not enough. More for Mitch. He can hardly glug all that milk down, but he still wants more. Most human beings would choke trying to drink down all of that milk. More glug. *Glug. Slurp, slurp. Clunk. Glug, glug.* What is a gulag?

Oh, it's Russian. Is a gulag like a glug of milk? No. But there is something like a gulag in America in 2019.

A Border Gulag. A gulag is a detention camp. A concentration camp. A place with a big fence to pen up human beings like cows, but less than cows. Careless. Care less. Humans, but treated inhumanely[1]. Like moo cows, but less. Like cashcows, but less. *Glug, glug.* Does caging human beings create money like the cashcows? In a way. But that is not the main point of caging them in. The main point is to assert **power**. Moscow Mitch likes **power. Pow, pow.** Moscow **power.** Blocks and blocks of **power.** *Clunk.*

1   Rappleye, H. and Riordan Seville, L. (2019). 24 immigrants have died in ICE custody during the Trump administration. [online] NBC News. Available at: https://www.nbcnews.com/politics/ immigration/24-immigrants-have-died-ice-custody-during-trump-administration-n1015291 [Accessed 24 Sep. 2019].

2

Moscow Mitch sells to the highest bidder. Rusal. Rusal wants to open an aluminum plant in Kentucky. Kentucky, Kentucky, chickens. Fancy farm. Moscow Mitch's home state. Tincans. Cashcow. *Moo*. Milk. Suddenly, Moscow Mitch cockblocked security laws. Protecting American elections against foreign attacks[2]. Why cockblock? *Cock-a-doodle-doo!*

Moscow **power**. Blocks and blocks of **power**. **Power** is **power**. Moscow Mitch is a Moscow Mitch. Moscow Mitch wants **power** as much as he wants

---

2 As of September 19, 2019, McConnell changed his tune on some election security. Sonmez, F. and Werner, E. (2019). In turnaround, McConnell backs $250 million in election security funding. [online] washingtonpost.com. Available at: https://www.washingtonpost.com/politics/in-turnaround-mcconnell-backs-250-million-in-election-security-funding/2019/09/19/b9f64462-daec-11e9-ac63-3016711543fe_story.html [Accessed 23 Sep. 2019].

cashcows mooing and milking. **Gold**. **Gold** and more **gold**. *Clunk*. *Clunk*. *Clunk*. Into the milk pail. The overflowing milk pail. Moscow **pow**. Moscow **power**. Moscow Mitch likes **power**. **Pow**!

Rusal said, "Here's some **power**. You block people from stopping our investment, and we'll do business in your home state with $200 million." Moscow Mitch is a Moscow Mitch. He had his top underlings lobbying Congress. "Let the good Russians invest in American aluminum," they said. 200 million cashcows. *Moo, moo*. **Gold** is good. *Clunk, clunk*. Blocks of **power**. Blocks of Moscow **power**.

Those underlings were powerful. Even though they were once under Moscow Mitch. Down under. Underneath. Under like an udder. Udder. Cow teats. *Moo*. Moscow Mitch. Mitch's bitches. Chief of staff, Hunter Bates. Hunt, hunt! Top adviser, Brennan Dunn. One and done, done. Moscow Mitch is rich. Rich =

Power. Powder. Powder keg. Blow those sanctions away. **Pow**!

But another piece was in place. US Treasury Department head, Steve Mnuchin. Trumpo's little buddy, Mnuchin. Greenlights. Grinning. Lighting. Greenlighting the powder keg to blow the sanctions away. Grinning, grinning. Hunting. All done. Done and done. **Gold**. *Clunk, clunk, clunk.*

Congress bows and rolls on its back. *Whine*. More of Mitch's bitches. Roll back. Rollback those Russian sanctions. It's OK. It's done. Dunn asked for done. It was done. Hunter hunted for done. It was hunted, found, and done. Those sanctions were abated, ended. Hunter Bates. Brennan Dunn. All abates, one and done. Moscow Mitch's underlings. Using their fingers to milk the cashcow teats into the pail. *Crack, crack. Clunk*. **Gold**.

3

Moscow **power**. President, Vladimir Putin. Oligarch, Oleg Deripaska. A president and his buddy. Big Moscow **power. Pow. Pow. Pow**! What is an oligarch? It's having undue political power. It's also having many cashcows. Due. Do. And doo doo. Rusal is Deripaska's cashcow. *Moo, moo. Crack, crack, crack. Clunk, clunk.* To the mooing of $28 billion cashcows, once. **Gold, gold**, and more **gold**. **Gold** is **gold**. Big hillocks of **gold**. Even if the pile shrank to $3 billion, that's still a lot more than Moscow Mitch has. A lot more. **Gold. Power. Pow**. Moscow Mitch is Putin's bitch. Rusal was blocked out of America. Cockblocked because it was controlled by Deripaska. Cockblocked. Cocked, cocked. *Cock-a-doodle-doo!* Blocked, blocked.

What's wrong with Deripaska? What's the big deal? How about messing in an American election? Chicken poop everywhere. How about threatening the lives of business rivals? Barnyard lumps. How about taking part in racketeering and extortion? Pig shit. How about illegally wiretapping a government official? Donkey dumps everywhere, look out! Fancy farm.

But a *cock-a-doodle-doo* block can be crushed by cashcow blocks. Big, heavy cashcows. Crushing cocky *cock-a-doodle-doo* roosters. **Gold**. And more **gold**. **Gold** is one of the heaviest metals. Aluminum is one of the lighter metals. Magic. Magic, all. Making aluminum into gold. Magic! *Moo!* Tincans are **golden**.

Moscow Mitch is a Moscow Mitch. Moscow Mitch will sing for the cashcows. *Moo, moo.* Moscow Mitch will sing for Deripaska. *Moo, moo.* And he'll sing some more, too. *Moo, moo.* He'd like to be an oligarch, too. But he's still so small time. Only $22.5 million cashcows. A lot less than Deripaska's $3 billion. **Pow. Power. Power** grabbing. Blocks of **power**.

Crush that cockblock, open that sanction against Rusal. Rusal, Rusal. Rusal in the USA, all. All. All. Russian. Rusal. Ruse. A ruse was used. A ruse was used against all. A ruse was used against USA, all. Hey. Hey ho. A Moscow Mitch is a Moscow Mitch. He'll use his bitches, Hunter Bates and Brennan Dunn. Break that cockblock. Break it. Cashcows are heavy. **Gold. Gold** is one of the heaviest metals. A tincan cockblock is crushed under the weight of a **golden** cashcow. Crush. Crushed. Russian crush. A Moscow Mitch is a Moscow Mitch. Crushing. Using a Russian crutch. A ruse. A ruse against the USA, all. Rusal.

• • •

Why did Congress cow? Not a cashcow, not a milk cow — just a cow? A cowardly yellow cow. Breaking the Rusal sanctions. Why? Why now, yellow cow? Yell, yell. Yell at the callow cow, all. Why now? Why give up your **pow**, cow? Why give up your **power**, yellow cow? Are you going to let that Rusal Trojan horse in, yellow cow? Rusal ≠ USA, all. Callow. Yellow. Callow. Yellow. Congress. Not so savvy. Yell, yell. Why did Americans vote for a cowardly yellow cow, Congress? *Moo.*

Moscow Mitch is a Moscow Mitch. His favorite thing is to block, cockblock, block, squat, *splat, cock-a-doodle-doo*! He brags about it. Brag, brag, brag. What a big rooster. The only thing that stops his cockblocking is a cashcow. *Moo, moo.* **Gold**. *Slurp*. No cashcow? Then a *"Cock-a-doodle-doo* cockblock to you," laughs Moscow Mitch. Squatting. Roosting. Roosting on a perch looking down. Beady eyes. Squat. *Splat, splat. Cock-a-doodle-doo, cock-a-doodle-doo.* Ha ha. Roosters roosting. Rusal. Russians, all.

Before Moscow Mitch was a Moscow Mitch, he was a cockblock Mitch. Blocking Merrick Garland's 2016 nomination. Supreme Court. *Cock-a-doodle-doo, cock-a-doodle-doo*! Mitch is gonna block you!

Brag. Brag. "The best thing I've ever done," bragged Cockblock Mitch. His wrinkly turtle frown turned upsidedown. A smile can be scary. Down, down, down. America is in the Upsidedown. America now has racists, rapists on the Supreme Court, the White House. Just replace "c" for "p" and back again. Racist. Rapist. Kavanaugh. Kavanaugh. In the rightsideup it would be Kava*naught*. Naught, naught. Dud. Zed. Zit. Zero. Kava-NOT.

America has another one for president, another zero, dud, zed, naught. Dreadnought. Teflon. Trumpo. Dreadnought. Teflon. In the Upsidedown. Down, down, down. How far down, America? *Cock-a-doodle-do!* **Pow**. **Pow**. **Power**. Cockblock Mitch grins, his turtle frown upsidedown, upsidedown. **Pow**. Smiles can be scary.

Cockblock Mitch is a Moscow Mitch. Blocking US election security. Rusal. Ruse for all. Starting in Kentucky. *Cluck, cluck. Peck, peck.* Moscow Mitch chuckles. **Gold**. *Slurp, slurp*. **Gold** and more **gold**. Moscow Mitch chuckles and turns that wrinkly turtle frown upsidedown. **Power**.

Moscow Mitch takes campaign contributions. From voting machine lobbyists. *Fiddle dee dee, fiddle dee dum*. Donating. Done. $4,000. *Peck, peck. Cluck, cluck*. Chickenfeed. Scatter. Chatter. What happened? Moscow Mitch blocked American election security bills. Cockblock. *Cluck, cluck*. The day after former special counsel Robert Mueller warned, all. Warned of Russian sabotage. Russian sabotage. Election meddling. Chicken poop everywhere. *Cluck, cluck*. Fancy farm.

Len Blavatnik. A Russian-born U.K./U.S. citizen. Or is he Ukrainian? Huh. *Sir* Len Blavatnik. Little buddies with Oleg Deripaska. 22.5% ownership of Rusal, all. Lenny owns 22.5% of Rusal. Estimated worth $21.2 billion. **Gold**. **Gold**. **Gold**. Where's Mitch's PAC cashcow, Lenny? $3.5 million. $3.5 million, all. That's a heavy cashcow. **Gold**. *Moo, moo*. Moscow Mitch said, "Thanks Lenny. I'll cockblock that election security bill now." *Cock-a-doodle-doo*! Block, block. *Splat*.

5 Moscow Mitch is a Moscow Mitch. His wife is Elaine Chao! Elaine Lan Chao! Chao, chaos! Fancy farm chaos! How? Nepotism. Nominated by Trumpo. A Moscow Mitch is Trumpo's little buddy. Head pats. Good doggie. *Whine, whine.* Who is US Secretary of Transportation? Elaine Lan Chao!

Chao gave Kentucky chickens $80 million cash-cows! **Gold**. **Gold**. *Cluck, cluck. Moo.* Fancy farm chaos. Fancy farm Chao is a fancy farm chaos! Chao approves special Kentucky DOT projects! Moscow Mitch stays in office. Voters like special treats from Chao! *Cluck, cluck.* Dot, dot. Connect the dots. DOT to Kentucky. Special barnyard treats, just for Kentucky. Thanks, Elaine! *Yum!* $80 million, all. $80 million in barnyard treats for Kentucky. From Chao! **Pow,**

pow. **Power**. Chaos! But sometimes one thing means another. Chao, chaos! Bait-and-switch. Switch that bait. Done. Done and done. Chaos!

A Moscow Mitch is a Moscow Mitch. DOT cash for Kentucky coal miners? Pensions, health care, new development? Not. Not. Connect the dots, all. Connect the dots. Dot. DOT. Dot. DOT. That money goes to Rusal, Rusal in the USA, all. Tincans are **gold**. Aluminum is one of the lighter metals. **Gold** is one of the heavier metals. Who is US Secretary of Transportation? Elaine Lan Chao! Chao, chaos! **Pow**. A Moscow Mitch's wife. No pensions for Kentucky coal miners. Rusal needs that cashcow. *Moo*.

A Moscow Mitch says to Trumpo, "Nominate my wife. Keep me in office. I'll scratch your back." Trumpo goes, "Sure thing little buddy. Sure thing. But you're gonna have to scratch that back long and hard. You're gonna have to cockblock, when I tell you to, Mitchy." Okey dokey. A Moscow Mitch knows how to butter his bread. Butter, butter, churn that butter. Moo cows make milk and milk makes butter. Butter goes on bread. A Moscow Mitch knows how to do a long and hard cockblock. *Scritch, scratch.* Block. Block. **Pow**. A Moscow Mitch is Trumpo's little buddy.

Moscow Mitch has a brother-in-law, Jim Breyer. Hey ho. *Bray, bray.* Jim Breyer is no donkey, hey, hey. He's just a simple venture capitalist. Hey, ho. *Bray.* But he likes cashcows, too. *Moo.* **Gold**. He gave a nice cashcow to his brother-in-law Moscow Mitch. He also likes Russia. Ruse, ruse. Jim Breyer, all. He invested a lot with one of Putin's little buddies, Yuri Milner. Oh, just an investor in Facebook, all. Yuri Milner invested in Facebook. **Gold**. *Clunk.* Facebook disinformation, all. Fiddling with elections. Cambridge Analytica. Brexit. Exit. Data fiddling. *Fiddle dee dee, fiddle dee dum.* Fidget spinners. Spin that data. Fiddle it. *Spin, spin.*

Moscow Mitch turns his turtle frown upsidedown. "Think of me as the Grim Reaper," he said. Grim. Grins. Chuckles. Moscow Mitch is a Moscow Mitch. Moscow Mitch is a #MassacreMitch. One day in America, there are two mass shootings. *Bang, bang.* One in El Paso, Texas[3]. One in Dayton[4]. *Bang, bang.* Death. Dead. 22 people dead. Pointy heads, white sheets. Sheets. Seeds. Sheets. Seeds. Sow. Sowing. Little white seeds of hate. *Soo-ey*!!! Homegrown terrorism. Domestic ≠ safe. Massacre. Shooting. Then 31 people dead, lickety-split.

---

3 En.wikipedia.org. (2019). 2019 El Paso shooting. [online] Available at: https://en.wikipedia.org/wiki/2019_El_Paso_shooting [Accessed 23 Sep. 2019].
4 En.wikipedia.org. (2019). 2019 Dayton shooting. [online] Available at: https://en.wikipedia.org/wiki/2019_Dayton_shooting [Accessed 23 Sep. 2019].

More people dead than hours in a day. In less than a day. 31 dead within 14 hours. Gilroy Garlic Festival[5]. Gilroy, California, too. 3 dead there, too. Same week. Same week shooting. One week, 34 dead by 3 mass murderers in America. Moscow Mitch grins. Grim Reaper. Grim and grinning. Grin. It was a massacre, Mitch. What a little bitch.

A little NRA bitch. *Whine, whine*. #MassacreMitch turns his turtle frown upsidedown. Chuckles. Grinning. What kind of cashcow for cockblocking a Senate vote? NRA says, $1.26 million. **Gold**. *Moo, moo*.

Run a full background check on gun buyers? *"Nyet,"* says Moscow Mitch. NRA Cashcow = $1.26 million. *Moo, moo. Whine. Slurp*. **Gold**. Turns that turtle frown upsidedown, upsidedown. **Gold** turns that turtle frown upsidedown. America is in the Upsidedown. Death, death. A Moscow Mitch is a Grim Reap-

5   En.wikipedia.org. (2019). Gilroy Garlic Festival shooting. [online] Available at: https://en.wikipedia.org/wiki/Gilroy_Garlic_Festival_ shooting [Accessed 23 Sep. 2019].

er. Grinning, grins, grim, all. "I will be the Grim Reaper," he says. Grinning. Grim. Mitch. He said it. He said, "I will be the Grim Reaper." Tells who he is. Believe them when they tell you. Cockblocker.

• • •

A Moscow Mitch has his supporters. Some people. Moscow Mitch is a #MassacreMitch. Grim. He tweets his supporter's pictures. Twitter. Grin. One picture shows cardboard gravestones. Death markers. Cardboard gravestone says, "Amy McGrath". Democratic challenger, Amy McGrath. Death marker. 24 hours after the massacre of Americans in El Paso, in Dayton. Dead, death, dead, death. Tone-deaf, tone-dead. Death markers. Moscow Mitch is a formless squeal that does not end.

#MassacreMitch's website[6] says, "Kentucky Tough". Tough, huh? *Cluck, cluck.* Squat, *splat*. He

---

6   Mitch McConnell for U.S. Senate. (2019). Kentucky Tough - Mitch McConnell for U.S. Senate. [online] Available at: https://www. teammitch.com/kentucky-tough/ [Accessed 1 Aug. 2019].

posts a picture with a bunch of white boys, all. Tough, tough. Not rough to be a *cock-a-doodle-doo* when you can hide behind a cashcow. Not rough. Those boys are mauling. AOC[7]. Death marker. A picture on a cardboard cutout. AOC. Death marker. Kissing and groping and choking. Choke. Kiss. Grope. Nope. Little nots. Zeds. Zits. Zeros.

Just like the president, all. Just like Kavanaugh, all. Sow. Sowing. *Soo-ey*!!! Little white seeds of hate. Scattering, chattering. Sheet. Shit. Sheet. Shit. "Break me off a piece of that," says the caption. Little white pointy heads filled with hate. Break. Beak. Break. Beak. *Cluck, cluck*. Kentucky tough, chickens. *Cluck, cluck*. Kentucky tough, chicken shit. Go eat shit. Mitch grins. He's so grim. And he has a tough. Squat. *Splat, splat*. *Cluck, cluck*.

---

7 Alexandria Ocasio-Cortez, an American politician who serves as the U.S. Representative for New York's 14th congressional district.

A Moscow Mitch won't allow a vote. An emergency vote on HR8[8]. Congress can't vote, all. Cockblock Mitch. Squat, squat. Beady eyes. *Splat*. What a chicken shit. HR112[9], extend those background checks. Gun safety. Put the gun safety on. On, on. Come on. Put it on. Put the gun safety on. Common. C'mon. Common. C'mon. Common-sense. *Come on*! Extend the checks. It's common-sense. Unless you're a little NRA bitch. Right, Mitch? **Gold**. How much? $1.26 million.

---

8 **Bipartisan Background Checks Act of 2019**. Cite: Congress.gov. (2019). H.R.8 - 116th Congress (2019-2020): Bipartisan Background Checks Act of 2019. [online] Available at: https://www.congress.gov/bill/116th-congress/house-bill/8 [Accessed 23 Sep. 2019].

9 **Enhanced Background Checks Act of 2019**. Cite: Congress. gov. (2019). H.R.1112 - 116th Congress (2019-2020): Enhanced Background Checks Act of 2019. [online] Available at: https://www. congress.gov/bill/116th-congress/house-bill/1112 [Accessed 23 Sep. 2019].

But those are not the only bills that Moscow Mitch squats on. VAWA[10]. Anti-Corruption. Infrastructure. Paycheck fairness. Net neutrality. Election security Bills, bills, bills. Not beaks. Not breaks. But bills. More bills. Over 100 bills. Not duck beaks. Bills. Ducking[11] the bills. Waiting for a senate vote. Waiting to pass. Moscow Mitch ducks the bills. *Quack*. Duck and hide. Duck hide. Duck blind. Shooting happens from a duck blind. *Bang*. Why do the blind lead the blind, Mitch? Hide, hide. *Quack. Quack.* What's Moscow Mitch ducking now? Bills. Hide. Hide from big buddy Trumpo, don't make him mad! Frown, frown, your smile is upsidedown.

They are not eggs, Mitch. You don't have to sit on them. HR 8, HR 112. VAWA, Anti-Corruption bills. They aren't eggs, Mitch. Let them hatch. They

---

10 H.R.1585 — Violence Against Women Reauthorization Act of 2019. Cite: Congress.gov. (2019). H.R.1585 - 116th Congress (2019-2020): Violence Against Women Reauthorization Act of 2019. [online] Available at: https://www.congress.gov/bill/116th-congress/house-bill/1585 [Accessed 23 Sep. 2019].

11 What rhymes with "ducking"? Yup, He's doing that to the bills, too.

want to hatch, open, breathe. Open up. Get off the nest, Mitch. *Cluck, cluck. Splat*. Grim. Grinning. Grim Reaper. Moscow Mitch. Beady eyes. Squat. *Splat. Splat*. A Moscow Mitch is Trumpo's little buddy. What a chicken shit.

"I'll let it peter out." Moscow Mitch said. "If I sit on those eggs, they'll just die. I won't let them pass. Smother 'em." Grins. Amazing that Mitch can spread his ass to fit over all of those eggs. Over 100 eggs. Egg. Clegg[12]. Egg, clegg. Clegg those eggs. Clegg 'em. Most chickens can only sit on about 12-15 eggs. Grim. Grin. Grim. Grin. Grim Reaper. Peter out. Peter, Peter, pumpkin eater. *Fiddle dee dee, fiddle dee dum*. "Big Buddy Trumpo doesn't want me to open the vote, so I'll squat on those eggs. SMother 'em." Grins. Cock-

---

12 To Clegg is to betray everything you once stood for in a dash of opportunism and stupidity. Cite: AshamedToHaveVotedLibDem (2010). Urban Dictionary: Clegg. [online] Urban Dictionary. Available at: https://www.urbandictionary.com/define. php?term=Clegg [Accessed 23 Sep. 2019].

blocker. Grim Reaper. Moscow Mitch. Grim. Grins. A smile can be scary.

• • •

It's on the USA fancy farm, all. Kentucky tough and chicken shit. What is chicken shit? It's hard to scrape off your boots. Dirt. Chicken dirt. **Gold**. Some NRA **pow**. **Power**. **Gold**. Some Russian **pow**. **Power**. **Gold**. *Moo, cluck, cluck*. Dirtbags gonna dirt, all. Dirtbags gonna dirt. NRA wants everyone to hurt. Why? Why else. Cashcows. *Moo*. **Gold**. **Gold. Gold**. Russians want everyone to hurt. Why? **Pow**. **Power**. **Pow**. **Power**. **Pow**.

Epilogue

"...here is my commitment: no matter how much they lie or how much they bully, I will not be intimidated...I'm proud of my record; I'm proud it's right there in black and white and liars cannot gaslight it away."

—*Moscow Mitch's personal spoken statement*[13] *in response to being called #MoscowMitch*

Moscow Mitch is a Moscow Mitch is a Moscow Mitch.

A Moscow Mitch = Hypocrite Mitch. *Moo.*

---

13 Burris, S., Palma, S., Edwards, D. and Reed, B. (July 29, 2019). McConnell accuses Dems of gaslighting him on Russian interference — and then blames Obama for Russian interference. [online] Rawstory.com. Available at: https://www.rawstory. com/2019/07/mcconnell-accuses-dems-of-gaslighting-him-on-russian-interference-and-then-blames-obama-for-russian-interference/ [Accessed 4 August. 2019].

www.ingramcontent.com/pod-product-compliance
Lightning Source LLC
Chambersburg PA
CBHW021948040426
42448CB00008B/1305